Dr. Seuss on the Loose!

It's Fun to Have Fun

"Look at me! Look at me!
Look at me NOW!
It is fun to have fun
But you have to know how.
I can hold up the cup
And the milk and the cake!
I can hold up these books!
And the fish on a rake!
I can hold the toy ship
And a little toy man!
And look! With my tail
I can hold a red fan!
I can fan with the fan
As I hop on the ball!
But that is not all.
Oh, no. That is not all…"

– *The Cat in the Hat*

Thinks to Think About

You can think up some birds.
That's what you can do.
You can think about yellow
Or think about blue.
You can think about red.
You can think about pink.
You can think up a horse.
Oh, the THINKS you can think!

– Oh the Thinks You Can Think!

How to Tell a Klotz From a Glotz

Well, the Glotz, you will notice,
Has lots of black spots.
The Klotz is quite different
With lots of black dots.
But the big problem is
That the spots on a Glotz
Are about the same size
As the dots on a Klotz.
So you first have to spot
Who the one with the dots is.
Then it's easy to tell
Who the Klotz or the Glotz is.

– Oh Say Can You Say?

On Eating Green Eggs and Ham

I would not, could not, in a box.
I could not, would not, with a fox.
I will not eat them with a mouse.
I will not eat them in a house.
I will not eat them here or there.
I will not eat them anywhere.
I do not eat green eggs and ham.
I do not like them, Sam-I-am.

– Green Eggs and Ham

Two Vrooms Sweep Clean

Oh, the things you can find if you don't stay behind!
On a world near the sun live two brothers called Vrooms
Who, strangely enough, are built sort of like brooms
And they're stuck all alone up there high in the blue
And so, to kill time, just for something to do
Each one of these fellows takes turn with the other
In sweeping the dust off his world with his brother.

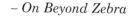

– *On Beyond Zebra*

What Made the Grinch so Grinchy?

The Grinch *hated* Christmas!
The whole Christmas season!
Now, please don't ask why.
No one quite knows the reason.
It could be his head wasn't screwed on just right.
It could be, perhaps, that his shoes were too tight.
But I think that the most likely reason of all
May have been that his heart was two sizes too small.

– How the Grinch Stole Christmas!

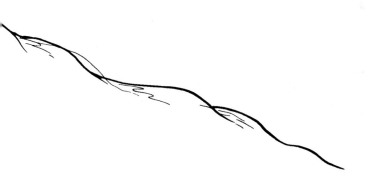

Tricks with Bricks and Chicks

And here's a
new trick, Mr. Knox…
Socks on chicks
and chicks on fox.
Fox on clocks
on bricks and blocks.
Bricks and blocks
on Knox on Box.

– *Fox in Socks*

Just Waiting...

Waiting for a train to go
or a bus to come, or a plane to go
or the mail to come, or the rain to go
or the phone to ring, or the snow to snow
or waiting around for a Yes or No
or waiting for their hair to grow.
Everyone is just waiting.

...aiting for the fish to bite
...r waiting for wind to fly a kite
...r waiting around for Friday night
...r waiting, perhaps, for their Uncle Jake
... a pot to boil, or a Better Break
... a string of pearls, or a pair of pants
... a wig with curls, or Another Chance.
...veryone is just waiting.

– Oh, The Places You'll Go!

Perfect Pets

I do not like this one so well.
All he does is yell, yell, yell.
I will not have this one about.
When he comes in I put him out.

This one is quiet as a mouse.
I like to have him in the house.

– One Fish, Two Fish
Red Fish, Blue Fish

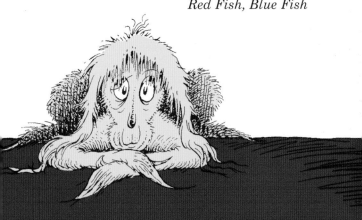

Battling Beetles
in a Bottle

When beetles fight these battles
in a bottle with their paddles
and the bottle's on a poodle
and the poodle's eating noodles...

…they call this
a muddle puddle tweetle poodle
beetle noodle bottle paddle battle.

– Fox in Socks

Taming the Beast

And now *Here*!
In this cage
Is a beast most ferocious
Who's known far and wide
As the Spotted Atrocious
Who growls, howls and yowls
The most bloodcurdling sounds
And each tooth in his mouth
Weighs at least sixty pounds
And he chews up and eats with the greatest of ease
Things like carpets and sidewalks and people and tre
But the great Colonel Sneelock is just the right kind
Of a man who can tame him. I'm sure he won't mind.

– *If I Ran the Circus*

Taking Time Out

Do you know where I found him?
You know where he was?
He was eating a cake in the tub!
Yes he was!
The hot water was on
And the cold water, too.
And I said to the cat,
"What a bad thing to do!"
"But I like to eat cake
In a tub," laughed the cat.
"You should try it some time,"
Laughed the cat as he sat.

– *The Cat in the Hat Comes Back*

Just Bobbing Along

FLOOB is for Floob-Boober-Bab-Boober-Bubs
Who bounce in the water like blubbery tubs.
They're no good to eat.
You can't cook 'em like steaks.
But they're handy in crossing small oceans and lakes.

– *On Beyond Zebra*

Time for Bed

Creatures are starting to think about rest.
Two Biffer-Baum Birds are now building their nest
They do it each night. And quite often I wonder
How they do this big job without making a blunder.
But that is *their* problem.
Not yours. And not mine.
They point is: They're going to bed.
And that's fine.

– Dr. Seuss's Sleep Book

Good Night

And now
good night.
It is time to sleep.
So we will sleep
with our pet Zeep.

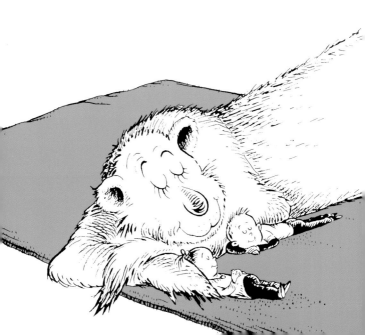

Today is gone. Today was fun.
Tomorrow is another one.
Every day,
from here to there,
funny things are everywhere.

– *One Fish, Two Fish, Red Fish, Blue Fish*

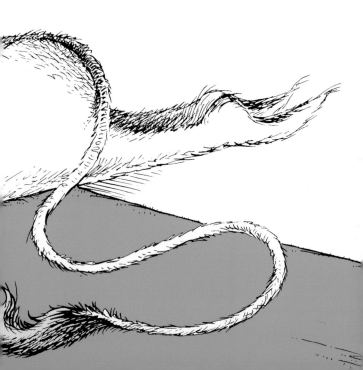

Dr. Seuss on the Loose!
™ & © 2008 by Dr. Seuss Enterprises, L.P.
All Rights Reserved

Original titles published by arrangement with
Random House Inc., New York, USA
This anthology published in the UK 2010 by
HarperCollins*Children's Books,*
a division of HarperCollins*Publishers* Ltd

The HarperCollins website address is:
www.harpercollins.co.uk

Printed and bound in China
2 4 6 8 10 9 7 5 3 1